Anonymus

First Annual Report of the Board of Trustees and Officers

Alabama Institution for the Education of the Deaf and Dumb

Anonymus

First Annual Report of the Board of Trustees and Officers
Alabama Institution for the Education of the Deaf and Dumb

ISBN/EAN: 9783741177804

Manufactured in Europe, USA, Canada, Australia, Japa

Cover: Foto ©Thomas Meinert / pixelio.de

Manufactured and distributed by brebook publishing software
(www.brebook.com)

Anonymus

First Annual Report of the Board of Trustees and Officers

FIRST ANNUAL REPORT

OF THE

BOARD OF TRUSTEES AND OFFICERS,

OF THE

ALABAMA INSTITUTION,

FOR THE

Education of the Deaf and Dumb,

LOCATED AT TALLADEGA,

TO THE

GOVERNOR OF THE STATE OF ALABAMA,

FOR THE YEAR ENDING

JULY 1, 1861.

———•——

MONTGOMERY:
MONTGOMERY ADVERTISER BOOK AND JOB PRINTING OFFICE.
1861.

DEAF AND DUMB ALPHABET.

a a   b b   c c   d d   e e

f f   g g   h h   i i   j j

k k   l l   m m   n n   o o

p p   q q   r r   s s   t t

u u   v v   w w   x x   y y

z z   & &

Institution for the Education of the Deaf and Dumb,

Talladega, Ala., July 1, 1861.

To His Excellency, Andrew B. Moore, Governor of Alabama:

I have the honor to present you herewith the First Annual Report of the Trustees and Officers of the Alabama Institution for the Deaf and Dumb.

With high Respect,
Your obedient servant,
W. TAYLOR,
Sec. of Board.

PRINCIPAL'S REPORT.

Gen. J. T. Bradford, President of Board of Trustees of Alabama Institution for Deaf and Dumb:

SIR:

In submitting to your body this, the first Annual Report of the Principal of the Alabama Institution for the Deaf and Dumb, embracing the time from the establishment of the Institution, on its present basis, to date, we would express our devout thanks to Almighty God for His manifest mercies vouchsafed to the inmates of the Institution. It has been to us a season of health—not a single case of serious illness among the pupils; and upon the whole it has been a period of prosperity, notwithstanding the excited state of the public mind—"the wars and rumors of war" which have been and are still rife through the land. The diligence of our pupils and their progress in the acquisition of useful knowledge, has been in some cases, highly gratifying, and in all cases satisfactory.

The number of pupils in attendance during the time specified, has been twenty-six. With this we hand you a list of their names, places of residence, &c. This number appears quite small when we remember what our State can furnish and who should be the recipients of her benefaction.

As this is the first Annual Report which has gone forth to the public, we propose giving a succinct account of the incipiency of the Institution and its after progress; and as it will probably fall into the hands of many who are interested in its success and would be gratified in the possession of the means of extending its usefulness, we propose adding such information as will aid in the accomplishment of that purpose.

community, salubrity in climate, and accessibility of location, present inducements for an Institution of this character, we cannot believe that the town of Talladega can be surpassed by any town within the limits of the State.

The improvements on the premises, consisted of a main building, and one or two small wooden buildings contiguous. Of the main building we would remark that it was built in the most substantial manner, after the Corinthian style of Architecture. It consists of three stories and a garret, with a beautifully collonaded front. The building having been specially designed for a female school, of course it is not adapted in all its appointments to the requirements of a mixed school of this character. The necessary alterations can be made by a small outlay of money, which we are confident the liberality of our Legislature will cheerfully grant. Under the existing arrangement the several rooms of the ground floor are appropriated to a dining hall, an ironing room, and to a workshop; the second floor to the school-room, and to sleeping apartments for the officers of the Institution; the third floor to the sleeping apartments of the pupils. The garret is at present unoccupied.

The property, when purchased by the State, was not in good condition. The fencing was broken down in many places, and the roof, the steps and windows considerably out of repair.

We have had the entire grounds enclosed with a substantial planking, and have had the portion fronting the street, together with the garden neatly and substantially paled. We have also had the lawn in front set in elms, maples, oaks, and other trees, in such a manner as to give promise of beauty in the adornment, and of healthful, invigorating shade. It is our purpose to have the whole set in some perennial grass. The intention has been and will continue to influence us in these improvements to adapt the whole to the physical and intellectual well-being of the inmates of the Institution. For, whatever captivates the eye, if properly directed, necessarily enlarges knowledge, elevates the character, and gives the mind resources within itself, which are peculiarly valuable to those whose calamity often deprives them of a full share of that mental occupation derived from social intercourse.

The undersigned having been appointed Principal, he submitted in nomination, for the office of Assistant Teacher, Miss

Sarah F Johnson; for Steward and Matron, Mr. R. R. Asbury and his wife, Mrs. C. B. Asbury; and for Superintendent of Shoe Shop, Mr. E. M. Houghston. These nominations were duly confirmed by the board. The same corps of officers still hold their respective positions, and whatever of doubt, if any may have existed, as to their fidelity and efficiency, has been entirely dissipated. We can and do unhesitatingly say that they have been faithful in the discharge of duty, watchful over their charge, and kind and affectionate in their intercourse with the pupils.

In connection with the Institution we have also opened a Shoe Shop, the design of which is to encourage habits of industry in our pupils, and to qualify them for self dependence, when they leave our care. It will be remembered that a large majority of our pupils are in indigent circumstances. Our efforts to ameliorate their condition would be wanting in much of practical utility if we should fail to teach their hands to labor, that they may be able to earn their support, and not be drones in society. We, by this means, practically impress upon their minds a wholesome, but too often neglected truth—*that labor is honorable.* Under a sense of its utility and importance the Legislature granted the sum of one thousand dollars for the purpose of erecting shops, &c. As several hundred dollars of this was needed in procuring an outfit, and as a room on the ground floor of the main building could, by changes in construction, be used temporarily for shop purposes, we have used only so much of this fund as was needed, and have held the balance in abeyance until such time as an additional sum can be secured, which will enable us to place the mechanical department upon a footing to fully meet the wants of the Institution.

An account of the present condition of the Institution would be incomplete if we should neglect to mention its wants, and submit such suggestions as would, in our judgment, materially promote its prosperity. It is known to your body that repeated abortive efforts have been made to procure a supply of water, by sinking wells on the premises. The peculiar geological formation of the grounds of the Institution, almost forbid the hope of finding water at a convenient depth. To remedy this natural defect a cistern had been constructed near the main building, and was in good condition when the property was purchased. This cistern, by using economy, has not supplied us fully with water. And as we look forward to an increase in our numbers, we regard the construction of another cistern of equal dimensions, as an act of immediate necessity.

The roof of the Main building is constructed of shingles and, as such, is liable at any time to be consumed by fire. In its present condition the insurance on it would be high. Aside from these prudential considerations the dictate of humanity requires that the lives of the unfortunate inmates should be shielded, as far as practicable from the dangers of fire. Their peculiar misfortune augments their liability to injury in cases of accidents of this kind. We then respectfully suggest that one of the wants of the Institution, is the substitution of some fire-proof material for a roof, in place of the highly inflammable material of which the present roof is composed.

We have had our grounds enclosed with a substantial railing and paling. This, together with the outbuildings, should be protected from decay by being well painted. Would not true economy suggest that as paint will add perhaps fifty per cent. to their durability, such a thing should be done at the earliest practical moment?

Last, under the head of *wants*, we would respectfully submit the propriety of making such changes in the internal arrangement of the building as will better adapt it to our purposes. This can be effected at a small cost; and in effecting the change a convenient opportunity will be afforded for the introduction of gas light into the building. The importance of this latter improvement will at once present itself, when the Board remembers that the class intended to be benefitted, are dependent solely upon the eye for all of happiness this life can afford them. The dim light of candles or of oil, must tax the eye in a greater or less degree, and to that extent impair its powers. There certainly could not be any objection to the introduction of gas light except it be on the score of economy. The appliances for its generation are now so simple and cheap, we strongly incline to the opinion that on investigation of the subject, economy will point to such a wished for consummation.

We have not given specifically the probable cost of the several *wants* we have enumerated, but feel quite confident that the sum already appropriated for the benefit of the Deaf and Dumb, if placed in the hands of the Board of Commissioners, will be sufficient to meet the entire expense. We would then suggest that the control of said sum be solicited at the next General Assembly, to be used at the discretion of the Board.

When it is remembered that there are within the limits of the State not less than one hundred persons, who could of right avail themselves of the State benefaction, and should be its recipients, it may be a matter of surprise, that more are not in attendance upon the exercises of this Institution. There are several reasons for this condition of things, some of which, whilst they should not exist, are creditable to our nature; and there are others which, whilst they do exist, are not so creditable. A wise and beneficent Providence has implanted in the parental heart a strong attachment for offspring. When that offspring is physically or mentally defective the feelings of the parent's heart are augmented in proportion to the magnitude of the defect. These feelings, unless controlled by the powers of a well balanced mind soon become morbid ; and not unfrequently when the parent is asked to commit his child to the care of strangers, they induce him to believe that *he will receive ill usage, because of his very misfortune*. However creditable to the heart this excessive affection may be, it has not unfrequently condemned many an unfortunate one to grope his way in silent darkness from the cradle to the grave. We infer from this fact that it is highly important to remove from the parent's mind every obstacle to a cheerful assent to placing his child under instruction. How stands the case with our institution? Have we removed every obstacle? We think not? We require the parents to clothe their children. Aside from the apparent narrowness of such a requisition, we submit that the policy is wrong, if not in theory, certainly in practice. If the evil fell upon the parent we would urge no change in the regulation, but it is for the sake of the innocent and unoffending that we would have the change made. As it now stands the regulation is made the pretext in too many cases, for the indulgence of the morbid feeling of which we have just spoken and a pretext in such cases, is all that is needed to make the feeling all controlling. In addition to this there are some who are unable, or if able, unwilling to furnish the requisite clothing. There have been those in our own Institution, who have been clothed in part, at least, by the kindness of others.

Notwithstanding this school has been in successful operation for nearly three years, and we have embraced every opportunity, both public and private, to make known the fact; yet we venture the assertion that not one tenth man in Alabama knows of its existence. A very large majority of those who should be informed are in indigent circumstances, and are generally illiterate. There is no way of reaching them so successfully, as by sending an agent into every nook and corner of the State, charged with the special duty of hunting up these children, and of urging upon their parents the importance of having them educated. This plan has proved effectual in other Institutions, and we doubt not would be equally so with us if adopted.

A very pertinent inquiry may be made of us in this connection, and one too which we take great pleasure in answering, as it affords us an opportunity to give information, which is not generally known. What is the real condition of the uneducated deaf mute, and to what extent does this misfortune go? However comprehensive the scope of the interrogatory we will venture in reply, a few of the many points of interest, trusting that by so doing, inquiry and investigation will be elicited to a point far beyond the limits prescribed in a mere outline Report.

It is exceedingly difficult for those of us who are in the full possession of all our powers of mind and body, to fully realize our feelings on being deprived of any one of them. In their free exercise we delight to revel in the bright sunshine—to roam amid the beauties of spring—to inhale the rich fragrance of summer—to contemplate the "sere and yellow leaf" of Autumn, and in winter to enjoy to satiety the abundance with which a smiling Providence has blessed us. We are capable, even in infancy, of smiling gratefully upon the hand that lends our tottering footsteps, and of imploring blessings upon the heart that points out to our wandering vision the evidences of creative power by which we are surrounded, and bids us look beyond these evidences to that uncreated spirit, which is the source of all power. As years roll on, the scope of our mental vision is enlarged, until, in the strength of maturity, we are capable of grasping many of the hitherto mysterious changes in visible objects, until we can comprehend the varied and ever varying aspect of the heavens above, and calculate with unerring precision, the metes and bounds of each returning season. And when, in the lapse of time our eyes grow dim with age, and our physical frames become shrunken and attenuated, we can look unappalled upon the approach of the great change which announces to us that this life has reached its appointed end. Such is the condition attainable by man in the full and vigorous possession, and exercise of the physical and mental gifts of God.

Not so, however, with those who are deprived of the powers of hearing and of speech—powers so essential to man's proper mental development. Imagine, if we can, their condition. Emphatically children of silence, they are cut off from all the charms and improvement of social intercourse. The bright fields and waving groves may echo the notes of the feathered songster, yet they heed them not. The gleeful songs of childhood excite not a feeling in their imprisoned minds. The voice of affection, though falling from a mother's sacred lips, excites no emotions in their unimpressed hearts: yea! the thunder's voice awakes no echo in their dead ears. Confined to the narrow horizon of vision their thoughts are dwarfed in the conception, and unaided, struggle in vain, to rise above the lowest heathen in their efforts to comprehend the grand and the beautiful. To them no light of truth has been sent; and for them the handiwork of God has no power to excite mental activity, or to create an idea of moral responsibility. They drag the lengthening chain of life day by day, from the cradle to the grave. And when life with them is ended, they sink with unutterable horror into (as they regard it) the abyss of annihilation.

If all this be true, and we think that an intimate association of more than fifteen years with many of these unfortunate ones, justifies us in pronouncing the picture not overdrawn, we ask if there lives a man in all the bounds of our State, in whose heart lingers a single spark of sympathy for the sufferings of our race, who would withhold from these children of misfortune all the comforts which this life can afford them? These minds are not hopelessly imprisoned. They are not hopelessly doomed to ignorance—to grope their way in darkness from their mother's arms to the cold embrace of death. They can be rescued: their fetters can be unloosed, and they be permitted to walk forth as companions with the most gifted of our race, and with them, revel in the boundless charms which nature yields to her votaries, comprehending with them the relations, and appreciating the responsibilities which man sustains to his fellow man, and with them rise to the majestic contemplation of the character and attributes of the Supreme Head of the universe.

The grand object of our Institution, is to effect just such a transformation in the lives of the many uneducated Deaf Mutes of our State; and we would appeal to every philanthropic heart to aid us in our purpose. We are sure our appeal will not be made in vain.

The census of the State informs us that there are over two hundred Deaf and Dumb persons in our limits. The number in all probability largely exceeds that sum. We are certainly in the bounds of a reasonable probability in saying that, at least one hundred of that number should of right be under instruction. Information from all parts of the State about such persons is earnestly solicited. Such information may prove but a cup of cold water to some thirsty, famishing soul. But let us remember that even a cup of cold water is remembered in the great day of accounts.

In concluding this report, you will Sir, permit the undersigned, in his own behalf, and in behalf of the officers and pupils of the Institution, to express our high appreciation of the unvarying urbanity of deportment, and of the unabated interest in our welfare evinced by the Board in their liberal views and actions in fostering the material prosperity of the Institution.

With this date we enter upon another year with hearts of thankfulness for blessings past, and of hopes of prosperity for years to come.

All of which is respectfully submitted.

JOS. H. JOHNSON, Principal.

July 1, 1861.

Steward's Report.

———◦•◦———

Gen. J. T. Bradford, President, &c.:

SIR:

As steward of the Ala. Institution for the Deaf and Dumb, I herewith transmit an abstract from my books, the accounts having been rendered quarterly and filed by the Secretary. Permit me in behalf of the Mutes to thank you, and through you, the Board, for the interest you have shown in their welfare and the promptness with which you have always acted.

Expenses of the 1st quarter ending April 1st, 1860							$834,73
"	"	" 2d	"	" July	"	"	668,36
"	"	" 3d	"	" Oct.	"	"	404,34
"	"	" 4th	"	" Jan.	"	1861	1280,61
"	"	" 1st	"	" April	"	"	776,46
"	"	" 2d	"	" July	"	"	627,46

All of which is respectfully submitted.

R. R. ASBURY, STEWARD.

Dr. Gabriel B. du Val, in Account with the Treas. Alabama Institution for the Deaf and Dumb. Cr.

Oct.	12	By amt. paid J. & J. B. Heney ...	70 80
"	12	" Miss S. F. Johnson	125 00
"	12	" E. M. Hughston	75 00
"	27	" R. R. Asbury	90 00
Nov.	15	" R. R. Asbury	100 00
"	15	" A. Bingham	107 00
1861.			
Jan.	14	" R. R. Asbury	2,030 61
April	9	" R. R. Asbury	1,436 33
July	6	" R. R. Asbury	750 00
Aug.	27	" R. R. Asbury	487 46
Aug.	27	By amount to balance	2,084 31
			$31,000 00

$31,000 00

$2,084 31

1861.			
Aug.	22	To balance brought down	$2,084 31

2

Report of the Trustees

Alabama Institution for the Deaf and Dumb.

The Board of Trustees of the Alabama Institution for the
Deaf and Dumb, by their Secretary, beg leave to submit
their first Annual Report.

The Legislature of the State of Alabama at its session of
1859, '60, passed an act for the establishment of an Institution
for the education of the Deaf and Dumb children of the State.

For the accomplishment of this object, Gabriel B. du Val,
the Superintendent of Public Education in the State and his
successors in office, together with four other persons to be nominated by the Governor and confirmed by the Senate, were created a body corporate with right of succession forever, by the
name of "The Alabama Institution for the Deaf and
Dumb." These Trustees or Commissioners in addition to other
powers incident to their appointment, were vested with the
power to locate said Institution and purchase a site therefor,
together with the necessary buildings, or cause the same to be
erected.

The sum of twenty thousand dollars was appropriated for the
purchase of a suitable situation and buildings for said Institution,
or for the purchase of a situation, and the erection of suitable
buildings.

An annual appropriation of five thousand dollars was also
made for the support of said Institution.

The said Trustees were also authorized to establish a
____ department in connection with said Institution

(the nature of which to be determined by the Board) in which the male pupils should receive instruction. For this purpose a further sum of one thousand dollars was appropriated and placed at the disposal of the Board.

This act to establish "The Alabama Institution for the Deaf and Dumb," was approved by the Governor on the 20th day of January, 1860. In pursuance of said act, the following Commissioners or Trustees were nominated and confirmed. Gen. Jacob T. Bradford, Hon. James B. Martin, Marcus H. Cruikshank, Esq., and Dr. William Taylor.

This Board of Commissioners with G. B. du Val, Esq., Superintendent of Education for the State, met at Talladega, Ala., on the 4th day of February, 1860, and organized by the appointment of Gen. J. T. Bradford, President, and Dr. William Taylor, Secretary of the Board ; Mr. du Val being Treasurer, *ex officio*.

The Board decided to locate the Institution at the town of Talladega; and for that purpose effected a purchase of the buildings and grounds then occupied by the school for the Deaf and Dumb, and formerly known as "The East Alabama Masonic Female Institute." The price paid for the property was sixteen thousand dollars. The main building is a handsome and commodious structure of very superior brick work, three and a half stories in height, occupying an elevated position commanding a handsome view of the town, of beautiful and picturesque mountain scenery on the north and south, and of the fertile and cultivated valley on the east and west. The rooms are all well ventilated and as well arranged as any building not specially designed for the purpose. Some changes in the internal arrangement of the building might be advantageously made without much expense. And this we would recommend.

The out buildings consist of a kitchen, smoke-house, stables and other substantial frame buildings. The grounds, consisting of fourteen acres, are capable of being very handsomely improved and ornamented. The Board of Trustees consider the State very fortunate in securing this property. The location is altogether desirable, not only on account of its central position and accessibility by railroad communication, the moral and religious influence of the cultivated and refined population of the town and county surrounding it, but also in the great and important consideration of health. The entire immunity from disease or serious sickness of any character in the Institution since its establishment, is perhaps the best evidence of the healthfulness of the location.

The original cost of the buildings, constructed some ten years since, was over thirty thousand dollars. The roof, cornice, windows, hand railings, steps, &c., required repairs, and for this purpose the Commissioners expended the sum of nine hundred and twenty-five dollars. They also purchased eighty acres of woodland, lying some two miles from the Institution, for which they paid the sum of four hundred dollars.

The fencings and enclosures of the grounds were in very bad condition and had to be built entirely anew; for this purpose they appropriated the sum of eleven hundred dollars. For other permanent fixtures they paid the sum of two hundred and thirty-two dollars.

For furniture, bedding, bedsteads, &c., already in the building, they paid the sum of four hundred and eight dollars and ninety cents.

For additional furniture for the Institution, desks, clock, &c., they paid the sum of three hundred and twenty-four dollars and eighty-four cents.

For a horse, wagon and harness, they paid the sum of two hundred and thirty dollars, and for the traveling expenses of G. B. du Val, Treasurer, thirty dollars.

Leaving of the twenty thousand dollars appropriated for purchase and erection of buildings, a balance of one hundred and forty-one dollars and sixty-nine cents. This balance the Board expect to use in erecting a banistering to protect an exposure on the portico of the first story of the main building.

Suitable deeds have been executed for the real estate purchased, and they have been filed and recorded in the proper offices.

The Board established a mechanical department in connection with the Institution, in accordance with the design of the Legislature. They selected "Boot and Shoe making" as the trade best adapted to the purpose, of any single occupation, and one which could be established with as small an expense to the State as any other.

The amount appropriated to establish this department, (one

thousand dollars,) was not sufficient to erect a separate building for workshops and purchase tools and materials to start a shop. Two rooms in the basement of the building were therefore fitted up for the purpose.

The amount expended for the fitting up of shop, the purchase of tools, benches, leather and other materials for outfit up to date of this report, eleven hundred and six dollars and forty-four cents.

The Board employed an educated Deaf Mute, Mr. E. M. Hughston, to superintend and instruct the Mutes in this department; he is assisted by Mr. J. H. Jernigan, who is also an educated Mute, and both are superior mechanics. These gentlemen are boarded in the Institution and receive a salary of three hundred dollars each. Their salaries, to date of report, amount to the sum of five hundred and fifty dollars, making an aggregate expenditure of sixteen hundred and fifty-six dollars and forty-four cents.

To pay this expense, the sum of six hundred and forty-three dollars has been drawn from the appropriation of one thousand dollars made to establish the department, and the balance has been paid from the receipts of the shop. Leaving of the mechanical department fund unexpended, the sum of three hundred and fifty-seven dollars.

The entire receipts from the mechanical department to date, amount to the sum of eleven hundred and seventy-three dollars and forty-four cents.

From the partial experiment thus far made with this department, the Board feel confident that with the shops once erected, the department will be able to sustain itself.

The Board elected and employed the following officers of said Institution.

Dr. JOSEPH H. JOHNSON, Principal,
Miss SALLIE F. JOHNSON, Assistant,
Mr. REUBEN R. ASBURY, Steward,
Mrs. REUBEN R. ASBURY, Matron,

to whom they agreed to pay the following annual salaries:

Principal...............................	$1500 00
Assistant...............................	500 00
Steward...............................	700 00
Matron...............................	300 00
Making a total of.....................	$3000 00

The current expenses of the Institution commencing with the first session, 1860, and ending with the date of this report, July 1st, 1861, are as follows:

1860 April 1, T'ch'rs' and St'w'rds' salaries 1st qr.						$	750 00
" July "	"	"	"	"	2d "		750 00
" Oct. "	"	"	"	"	3d "		750 00
1861 Jan. "	"	"	"	"	4th "		750 00
" April "	"	"	"	"	1st "		750 00
" July "	"	"	"	"	2d "		750 00
							$4500 00
1860 April 1, St'w'd's ac'c't curr'nt exp'n's 1st qr.						$	788 26
" July "	"	"	"	"	"	"	582 23
" Oct. "	"	"	"	"	"	"	404 34
1861 Jan. "	"	"	"	"	"	"	905 61
" April "	"	"	"	"	"	"	686 33
" July "	"	"	"	"	"	"	627 46
							$3994 23
1860 Oct. 1, to amount paid advertising accounts,							90 00
" " " amount paid glazing accounts,							68 00
							$8552 23

To meet these expenses we have the following sums:

Annual appropriation 1860,	$5000 00
One half annual appropriation for 1861, (to July 1.)	2500 00
Cash received from pay pupils,	699 05
	$8199 05
Amount due from pay pupils, (unpaid.)	559 00
	$7186 05
Leaving a balance of	205 82

The Board of Trustees adopted a system of rules and regulations for the government of said Institution, which are too lengthy to be embraced in the report. They are full however, and well adapted to the government and regulation of all the different departments of the Institution.

Owing to the peculiar condition of the country, the Board feel reluctant to ask any additional appropriations for the benefit of the Institution. There are however some wants to be supplied, and some expenditures that even rigid economy would

require. The peculiar location of the Institution is such, that
water cannot be had by digging or boring wells except at
great expense. There is an excellent cistern which has supplied
the Institution with the very best water, but the supply is not
sufficient for the wants of the Institution. Another good cistern we deem almost an indispensable necessity. The kitchen,
smoke house and other wooden buildings ought to be painted for
their protection. The paling, immediately in front of the buildings, ought also to be painted. The present roof of the main
building, since the repairs, is water proof, but the risks from
fire with a roof of such combustible material, would require
that at the earliest practicable moment its place be supplied with
metal or slate.

The cheapness and facility with which gas can be generated
from pine, (which is abundant in the neighborhood,) would ren-
der it entirely practicable to light the Institution in that way.
Safety and convenience would require its adoption, and we
very much question whether economy would not also indicate
its introduction. The business portion of our town has been
lighted in that way for some time past.

The fund which was created for the purposes of Deaf Mute
education before the incorporation of the Institution, a portion
of which is now at interest, if placed at the disposal of the
Board of Trustees, would be ample to meet all these demands.

Shortly after the commencement of hostilities between the
government of the United States and the Confederate States,
Dr. Johnson, the principal of the Institution, raised a company
of twelve months volunteers and entered the service of the
Confederate States. He made arrangements to have his place
supplied by Prof. O. P. Fannin, late of the Georgia Institution
for the Deaf and Dumb. Prof. Fannin is an experienced and
competent teacher and has filled the position with perfect satis-
faction up to this time.

The Board will make arrangements to keep competent and
reliable teachers in charge of the Institution during Dr. Johnson's absence, and no effort shall be spared to keep every department under the best possible discipline and management.

The board take pleasure in saying, that thus far the management of the Institution in all the different departments has been
such as to meet their entire approval. The Mutes are neat in

their dress and appearance, and apparently happy and contented. The dormitories, recitation rooms and dining room are at all times found in perfect neatness and order. The most kind and parental attention is given to the pupils, and the yard and grounds about the buildings are kept in perfect order and always present a tasteful and cleanly appearance. The perfect harmony which has prevailed from the commencement of the Institution to the present time, shows that the trustees were most fortunate in the selection of teachers, steward and matron.

In the mechanical department the pupils have made rapid progress, and some of them can now do work that would pass creditably in the best established shops, and we take great pleasure in saying, that the teachers in this department have discharged their duties with great faithfulness.

The number of pupils in attendance, though quite as large as is usual in institutions of the same age, is small when compared with the number of Deaf Mutes in the State. A much larger number of pupils could be instructed in the Institution with but a small additional expense, and the Board would earnestly recommend the employment of some efficient agency to bring in those for whose benefit the Institution was especially designed, many of whom may not have heard of its existence. It being a well established fact that a large number of the Mutes are found in illiterate families.

Men of wealth in the State, some of whom we regret to say have heretofore patronized institutions in the northern states, will in the future from choice as well as necessity, be compelled to educate their children in the South, and we hope will find it to their interest to encourage the Institution established and fostered by the liberality of their own State. The advantages of the Institution will be inferior to none in the South, and state pride as well as self interest should prompt them to sustain and encourage our own Institution.

W. TAYLOR, Sec'y.

CATALOGUE OF PUPILS

Who have attended the exercises of the Institution to Date.

NAMES.	POST OFFICE.	CAUSE OF DEAFNESS.
John W. Brazil	Asbury, Ala	Accidental.
Francis M. Brooks	Greenville, Ala	Congenital.
Lucy C. Brooks	Greenville, Ala	Congenital.
Lewis B. Cargile	Stevenson, Ala	Accidental.
Benj. F. Canada	Eastaboga, Ala	Accidental.
Joseph A. Candler	New Site, Ala	Congenital.
Jeptha M. Fannin	Roanoke, Ala	Accidental.
George M. Franklin	Tallassee, Ala	Accidental.
Wiley T. Glover	Corn Grove, Ala	Unknown.
Mary E. Harlan	Pinckneyville, Ala	Congenital.
Aaron H. Harlan	Pinckneyville, Ala	Congenital.
Andrew J. Haws	Glennville, Ala	Congenital.
Lavina Haws	Glennville, Ala	Congenital.
William S. Johnson	Cave Spring, Ga	Congenital.
George C. Low	Union Springs, Ala	Congenital.
Mary E. McCarter	Talladega, Ala	Congenital.
Missouri McCarter	Talladega, Ala	Congenital.
Rufus C. Milford	Chamber's C. H. Ala	Unknown.
Maria C. Mimms	Prattville, Ala	Unknown.
Mary L. Owens	Butler, Ala	Congenital.
Henry V. Owens	Butler, Ala	Congenital.
John W. Patrick	Van Buren, Ala	Accidental.
Sarah L. Straughn	Burnt Corn, Ala	Congenital.
Mary E. Toney	Union Springs, Ala	Congenital.
Mary A. Wakefield	Alexandria, Ala	Congenital.
Andrew J. Willis	Rawlingsville, Ala	Congenital.
Minerva Yateman	Silver Run, Ala	Unknown.

Males .... 15 }
Females............................. 11 } 27

Paying Pupils....................... 8 }
Beneficiaries....................... 19 } 27

Trades taught at Institutions for the Deaf and Dumb.

CONFEDERATE STATES.

Virginia.—Shoemaking, Carpentry, Bookbinding, Braslma-king, Chairmaking, Printing for the Blind.

North Carolina.—Printing.

South Carolina.—Cabinetmaking, Shoemaking.

Tennessee.—Cabinetmaking, Shoemaking.

Georgia.—Shoemaking.

Mississippi.—Farming, Gardening.

UNITED STATES.

American Asylum.—Cabinetmaking, Shoemaking, Tailoring.

New York.—Cabinetmaking, Shoemaking, Tailoring, Book-binding, Gardening.

Pennsylvania.—Shoemaking, Tailoring.

Ohio.—Gardening.

Indiana.—Cabinetmaking, Shoemaking, Tailoring.

Illinois.—Cabinetmaking, Shoemaking, Gardening.

Wisconsin.—Cabinetmaking, Shoemaking.

Kentucky.—Shoemaking, Blacksmithing, Woodturning.

Missouri.—Farming, Gardening.

EUROPE.

Institution (Royal) at Paris.—Shoemaking, Tailoring, Join-ery, Woodturning, Blacksmithing, Lithographing.

Marseilles.—Cabinetmaking, Tailoring, Shoemaking, Litho-graphing.

Geneva.—Bookbinding, Printing, Embroidery.

Rome.—Shoemaking, Tailoring, Joinery, Statuary.

Vienna.—Cabinetmaking, Shoemaking, Tailoring, Printing, Woodturning.

Milan.—Shoemaking, Tailoring, Engraving.

Strasburg.—Shoemaking, Tailoring, Weaving, Carpentry, Gar-dening.

Brussels.—Shoemaking, Tailoring, Woodturning, Basketma-king, Baking.

Ghent.—Tailoring, Shoemaking, Joinery, Shaving and Hair-Dressing, Bottoming Chairs, Matmaking, Basketmaking, Bookbinding, Carpetweaving, Woodturning.

Edinburgh.—Shoemaking, Tailoring, Printing.

Doncaster.—Printing, Gardening.

ACKNOWLEDGMENT.

The following newspapers have been gratuitously sent to the Institute. We tender on the part of the Officers and pupils of the Institution, thanks to the editors and proprietors for this generous manifestation of their interest in and remembrance of the deaf mutes.

The Alabama Reporter, Talladega, Ala.
" Democratic Watchtower, Talladega, Ala.
" Confederation, Montgomery, Ala.
" Independent, Huntsville, Ala.

JAS. H. JOHNSON, PRINCIPAL.

TALLADEGA, JULY, 17, 1860.

Col. R. H. CHAPMAN.—*Dear Sir:*

I take pleasure in transmitting to you a copy of a resolution, adopted by the Board of Commissioners of the Alabama Institute for the Deaf and Dumb, at a meeting held this day :

"*Resolved*, That the Secretary tender to Col. R. H. Chapman the thanks of this Board, for the able and interesting address, delivered by him on last evening, and to request a copy for publication in our first annual report."

Hoping that it may suit your pleasure to comply with the expressed wish of the Board, I remain

Yours Truly,

W. TAYLOR, SECRETARY.

DR. W. TAYLOR, SECRETARY, &c.—*Dear Sir:*

Enclosed find copy of the address called for in your note of 17th July last. This address was hurriedly written, and I submit it for publication, more in the hope that the facts stated may be of some service to the cause of Deaf Mute instruction in this State, than from any original merit which I may imagine contained in it. If it is instrumental in exciting additional interest in behalf of the unfortunate, I shall consider myself fully compensated for the trouble of its composition.

Yours truly,

R. CHAPMAN.

Camden, Ala., Aug. 8, 1860.

ANNUAL ADDRESS,

Delivered by Col. Robert H. Chapman, of Wilcox.

—————————

It is a pleasant reflection that in this region, remarkable for the bitterness of its political discussions—the captiousness of its forensic contests—the acrimony of its religious controversies, and the decided and sometimes injudicious rivalry of its schools, that it is my lot to address you in behalf of a cause, respecting which there is no diversity of feeling or opinion.

I venture the assertion that there is not one in this assembly of the people of Talladega, nor of those here assembled from different parts of the State of Alabama, who does not desire that the amplest success may crown the efforts of the Alabama Institution for the Deaf and Dumb. There is not one who will not heartily say, God speed this enterprise, designed to ameliorate the condition of the unfortunate and elevate them in the scale of moral, social and religious being.

It has become the fashion to rail at the world and charge mankind with selfishness and want of feeling. As we are more apt to remember wrongs than benefits, so we note then with more particularity, and remember manifestations of harshness and cruelty with more distinctness, than we do deeds of kindness, benevolence and charity. Burns has said,

"Man's inhumanity to man makes countless thousands mourn,"

and the world has taken its text from Burns, overlooking what is equally true, that man's humanity and kindness to his fellow man, has made multitudes happy and scattered numberless blessings through all lands and among all peoples.

We might give many illustrations of the truth, that men are better than we give them credit for being; and that although when speaking of those undertakings which present human nature in its fairest light, we are obliged to confess that the "trail of the serpent is over them all," yet it is not unpleasing to meet frequent indications that the odors of Paradise are still hanging around many acts of the sons of Adam.

No other or better illustration need be given, than the establishment of this institution and institutions of like character in Europe and America.

To realize how much man has done for his fellow man deprived of the senses of hearing and speaking, we have but to look at the condition of the deaf mute before any effort has been made to admit light into his darkened understanding—before the kindly hand of his Instructor has rolled the stone away from the door of the sepulchre of his mind and soul. More unfortunate than the idiot, the deaf mute has sufficient intelligence to be sensible of the clouds which darken his intellect. His mental darkness is to him like the darkness of Egypt; he feels it, and though forever groping for light, his unaided efforts cannot enable him to dispel the night which surrounds him. He sees that his fellow-beings communicate in some mysterious way one with another; but how they do so is to him a painful enigma.

Familiar with the Geography of his native village or farm, he imagines nothing beyond the limited range of his vision. He knows nothing of the past, except as he remembers the events of his own life; he expects nothing in the future. He is ignorant of his own name and has no name for the most common objects around him. He knows nothing of the relations of father and mother, sister and brother; of family affections and ties of kindred, that highest link in the chain of human connections. He knows nothing of a God, of his soul, or of the immortality that awaits him. To him the voice of instruction, of friendship and of affection is addressed as to a senseless thing.

> "The Song of bird and bee,
> The chorus of breeze, streams and groves,
> All the grand music to which nature moves,
> Are wasted melody.
> To him the world of sound a fundess void,
> While even silence has its charms destroyed."

Until within the last fifty or seventy-five years, harsh legal enactments added injustice and artificial hardships to natural deprivations. The deaf mute was regarded legally as but a grade above the idiot. He could not inherit property, make contracts or marry. He was treated with rare exceptions, as an outcast by nature and accursed of God. In the midst of refinement and christianity, he was savage and heathen. The Hottentot or Digger Indian were rather to be envied than he, because the Hottentot and Digger were utterly ignorant of the existence of countless objects, which the eye had revealed to the deaf mute, but of which he could gain no knowledge by the workings of his own unaided intellect. Complete imbecility would have been bliss to the deaf mute. There would have been then no continual striving after the unattainable, and no constant disappointment on account of unavailing effort. Surrounded by every species of intellectual food, he was debarred the very crumbs of knowledge, and his mind gradually perished from absolute inactivity. Dependant on charity, the grudged assistance of others, he became morose and bad; an object of aversion and dislike as well as of contemptuous pity.

But now, ladies and gentlemen, having shown you the condition of the deaf mute in no darker colors than the facts of history portray it, let me reverse the picture. Since the establishment of schools for his instruction, we behold him a new creature. Now, owing to the judicious and kindly aid of his large hearted instructor—for that man or woman who devotes time, talents and life to the happiness of the unfortunate, must have a large heart—and owing to the establishment of such institutions as the Alabama Institution for the Deaf and Dumb, he can stand proudly up, a peer among his fellow men, feeling himself A MAN freed from the shackles which nature had imposed on his mind and body, "redeemed, regenerated and disenthralled," a fit being to bear the likeness of his God.

Practically restored by his teacher, in the prosecution of his God-like task, to the use of his dormant faculties, and taught some art or trade, he is no longer an incumbrance and a mere consumer of the fruit of other's industry; he is now independent and self reliant, begging alms from nobody; he makes his own living by his own labor, and may become no mean applicant for the prizes of life held out in the mental and physical world to the earnest and indefatigable worker.

He is now restored to full communion and has free interchange
of thoughts and feelings with his fellows. He understands and
appreciates his social relations. His teacher has given him an
insight into the higher elements of human character. Taught
him that man is designed and fitted, and that his chief enjoy-
ment consists in something higher and nobler than the mere
gratification of his animal nature. Made him to understand
and appreciate the operations of the mind, taught him reflection, and the connection of past, present and future. And
above all has made him to learn of Christ and to know of the
blissful realms where perfect happiness and fulness of joy
abound, and where his ears shall be opened, and the first
sounds received into his soul through his awakened senses shall
be his welcome into everlasting bliss, with the songs of the redeemed and the harpings of the glorified—the perfect melody
of the music of heaven.

> "When that new sense is given,
> What rapture will its first experience be,
> That never woke to meaner melody
> Than the rich songs of Heaven,
> To hear the full toned anthem swelling round,
> While angels teach the ecstacy of sound."

These representations of the condition of the deaf mute before and after receiving the instructions imparted by well quali-
fied teachers of the sign language, do not of course apply
to every case. Some deaf mutes when entirely untaught, manifest much intelligence, and some few are so stupid as not to be
taught successfully at all; but these are rare exceptions, and
in the main the above statement is neither overdrawn or exag-
gerated.

The teacher of the deaf and dumb has as a general rule, to
operate on a mind as blank as a sheet of paper, or at best
rather deformed by erroneous views of objects and things presented to his uninstructed vision. The first object of the
teacher is to think as the mute thinks; make him understand
by signs what is the character of the knowledge they have in
common.

The language of signs—pantomime—is the common language
in which they converse. The teacher improves on the mind of
the pupil by a thousand illustrations, the important and radical
fact that words are representatives of ideas. His ingenuity is

often taxed to find some expression by the signs for a particular idea. For this purpose he presents to the mute some familiar object such as a knife or a stick, and asks in the language of signs "what is this?" &c., varying the question to meet various phases of mental association. In this way by writing the name of the object on a blackboard or slate, the mute is led to associate the object with the particular combination of letters. To ensure success in fixing this idea, more advanced pupils are called in, and in presence of the beginner requested to point out the object when the name is referred to, and the name when the object is referred to. This will convey to the mind an idea, very imperfect it is true, of how deaf mute instruction is commenced and carried on, and also how important, in fact I may say absolutely, necessary to the attainment of any degree of perfectness in the art of deaf mute instruction it is, to have institutions of this sort where numbers are gathered together endeavoring to compass the same end. The other pupils furnish an example which incites the beginner to renewed effort, and the presence of numbers obliged to communicate by signs, quickens mental energies and gives confidence to the pupil, heretofore accustomed to associate alone with those who are perfect in the senses of hearing and speaking.

It was the establishment of institutions like the Alabama Institution for the Deaf and Dumb, which has caused such a revolution in the condition of the deaf mutes, and your attention is now directed to an account of the origin and progress of this art, which I shall endeavor to make as brief as possible. The materials for the preparation of such an account are very meager and my time has been very limited, but I hope I will be able to give a correct, general outline of the history of deaf mute instruction. Certainly I can promise, if you feel the same interest in this subject which every philanthropic heart should feel, it will not be found either uninteresting or uninstructive.

The first account we have of an effort to instruct the deaf and dumb, was about the beginning of the 16th century, in Spain.

Spain at that time was the most civilized nation in Europe. Her soldiers were the best; her generals the most skillful and able; her scholars the most profoundly learned, and her sover-

3

digns the wise t. In arts and sciences she excelled all others. At this age her enterprise had just afforded Columbus the means of discovering America and given a new world to Castile and Leon. All Europe since that period has enjoyed the fruits of her labor, while Spain herself, through bigotry and misrule, has reaped only misfortune and ruin from the very prosperity which her enterprise and her genius achieved.

The first instructor of whom we have any authentic information, was Peter Ponce, who taught two or three children of Spanish nobles about the beginning of the 16th century. Second in point of time was John Paul Bonet, the first who wrote a treatise on the art of instructing deaf mutes, also a Spaniard. Bonet employed the language of signs, the art of spelling on the fingers and writing. His work was published in 1620, more than one hundred years after the time of Ponce. The Cavalier Digby who accompanied Prince Charles and Geo. Villiers, afterwards the celebrated Duke of Buckingham, on their romantic expedition into Spain, speaks of a deaf mute, a pupil of Bonet, who, "though incapable to the report of a cannon, could distinguish the meaning of others by sight alone."

England in the 17th century presents us with the names of Bulwer, Wallis, Holder, Dalgarno and Sibscoth, all of whom directed their attention either to the theory or the practice of this art. Bulwer wrote a work on the subject in 1648. He was not an instructor himself, but endeavored to point out the proper path to others. He was the first to propose a system of instruction by means of signs. Wallis occupied the first rank among the early English instructors in the annals of deaf mute history. Many persons in Holland had their attention directed to this subject about the same period.

In Holland, however, as well as in Spain and England, the art fell into disuse after the time of its first inventors.

Early in the 18th Century, Kerner assisted by his sister, undertook the task of deaf mute instruction in Germany. He made use of the language of signs and his views were very similar to those of the Abbe De l'Epee, the celebrated French instructor of a later period in the same century, and who is justly styled the Father of deaf mute instruction. Kerner's enterprise unfortunately terminated with his life. Heinicke, of Saxony, was the Director of the first institution for the deaf and dumb, established under the patronage of a government. This institution was founded at Leipzig, in 1778.

This celebrated instructor while a member of the body guard of the Elector of Saxony, gave lessons about the year 1755 to a deaf and dumb boy. This experiment was interrupted by the seven years war. After the war he supported himself and wife by his skill in music, while pursuing his studies at the University at Jena. Several years afterwards, while teaching near Hamburg, he met with deaf mutes whom he instructed with such success, that his reputation came to the knowledge of the ———— Elector of ———— Saxony, to whom, first of all rulers, is due the praise of making provision for the support of a school for the deaf and dumb. By the invitation of this Prince, Heinicke removed his school to Leipzig in April, 1778. The institution thus founded furnished teachers and methods to the other early German schools; and the method of Heinicke, more or less modified, is still dominant throughout Germany. Between Heinicke and De l' Eppee a controversy arose on their respective systems, which divided the professors of the art of deaf mute instruction into two parties. It is foreign to our purpose to go into an account of this controversy. The great point at issue between them seems to have been the use of articulation or of sign language. Heinicke contending that it would be better to teach the deaf mute to articulate and understand another's words by the movements of the lips; while De l' Eppee contended that the use of natural and intelligible signs, was the better and more comprehensive method of conveying accurate conceptions and ideas to the deaf mute.

It is enough for our present purpose, that the views of De l' Eppee have been decided to have been most natural and philosophical, and that the methods invented and practiced by him, control and govern deaf mute instruction in this country, and that the triumphant success attending the efforts of his followers in America and Europe, have so far as we are concerned, decided the contest in favor of De l' Eppee.

Cotemporaneous with De l' Eppee and Heinicke, we find Braidwood undertaking the same work in Scotland; and it is a remarkable fact that these three instructors by their labors and success communicated the impulses to all the existing institutions for deaf mutes, each of whom with no knowledge of the labor of the others, had his attention drawn to this subject between the years 1755 and 1760.

Thos. Braidwood first commenced his labors in 1760, near Edinburg. It is supposed his school was located at, and gave the name to Dumbiedikes, a spot rendered classic by Walter Scott, in "The Heart of Mid Lothian." His school was afterwards moved to the neighborhood of London, and the institution thus founded by him is yet in successful operation under the control of his descendants, many of whom following the noble example of their ancestor, have from his time down to the present devoted themselves successfully to the same praiseworthy task.

A descendant of Thos. Braidwood removed to Virginia as early as 1811, and made the first effort to teach deaf mutes in America, but his greater devotion to alcoholic stimulants, brought to a speedy conclusion a career which promised to be useful and glorious. The Braidwoods, like Heinieke, made articulation the main object in instructing their pupils.

Until the advent of the Abbe De l' Eppee, France seems not only to have been behind other European nations in her efforts for the education of deaf mutes, but even in the knowledge of what had been accomplished abroad. Father Xavier had endeavored to teach two or three pupils by means of pictures. His death leaving his undertaking very incomplete, occasioned De l' Eppee to become accidentally acquainted with the deplorable condition of his pupils, and awakened his active sympathies in behalf of the deaf and dumb. De l' Eppee himself says, "The Father Xavier, a very worthy priest, had begun the education of two twin sisters who were deaf and dumb from birth. This christian minister being dead, the two poor girls found themselves without succor, no one having been willing during quite a long time to undertake the continuance or commencement of this work. Believing therefore that these children would live and die in ignorance of their religion if I did not essay some method to teach it to them, I was touched with compassion for them and said they might be brought to me, I would do all I could for them." Such was the modest beginning that has led to the rescue of such numbers from utter intellectual night and benefitted them above all appreciation; and this good work, so modestly storied by the benevolent and kind hearted Abbe, is still expanding and its prospects brightening.

Dr. Peet, in a report of the history of deaf mute instruction, to which we are largely indebted, speaks of De l' Eppee as follows: "De l' Eppee was at that time totally ignorant of the means used by the few teachers of deaf mutes who had preceded him, except Father Xavier with his pictures, which he remarks were not to his taste. The question says De l' Eppee, "was to lead my pupils to the understanding of words." Seekking for light in this new path, there came back to his recollection, as by inspiration, a lesson received in his youth from his teacher in philosophy, who proved to him that "there was no more necessary connection between metaphysical ideas and the articulated sounds that strike our ears, than between these same ideas and the written characters that strike our eyes;" and hence, "that it would be possible to instruct deaf mutes by written characters always accompanied by signs, as other men are taught by spoken words and gestures." Following out this vein of thought thus suggested, he bethought himself of the signs used naturally by deaf mutes, and conceived "that a method of combined signs should be the most convenient and surest way, as it could be equally applied to things absent or present, dependent or independent of sense."

That is, he first of all men, conceived the idea of a language of signs having its radicals in the natural language of gestures, but developed and extended on certain logical principles, till it should become in its vocabulary, its syntax and its inflection, so far parallel to speech, as to admit the task of instruction to be reduced to a mere translation of words into signs. The boldness of this conception under the circumstances, is remarkable. The teachers who preceded him had used natural signs more or less in the beginning; but none of them seem to have even suspected any extensive capability of cultivation or development in sign language. De l' Eppee, far beyond all others, is entitled to the gratitude of the deaf and dumb, not only as the originator of the only sensible and philosophical method of instruction, but because he urged the consideration of their unfortunate condition upon the attention of the world, in a light which appeals most strongly to benevolence and religious sympathy. In receipt of an income of $2000, he appropriated

——— to the support and education of his indigent pupils.
Teaching gratuitously, and devoting all his energies and his life
and fortune to the deaf and dumb, he was able in time to infuse
others with his own zeal to influence the establishment of other
schools for deaf mutes—the poor as well as the rich—and to
raise up numerous and zealous successors in the work to which
he had devoted himself. Other teachers had made a mystery
of their methods, and had endeavored to make their success a
means of improving their fortunes.

De l' Eppee, with heart and hand " open as day to melting
charity," looks beyond the attainment of a mere selfish end, or
the mere gratification of personal vanity and philosophical curi-
osity, to the present good and future happiness of the unfortunate outcasts, by nature or accident from their fellow men and
from their God. It required his great heart to give that im-
pulse to the cause of deaf mute instruction which comprehen-
ded the rich and the poor, the well born and the humble. It
is due to De l' Epee, that such institutions as the Alabama
Institution for the Deaf and Dumb are established, either by
private or public endowment, in nearly every country in Europe
and nearly every state in the Union.

The parent now, need not regard his deaf mute son or daughter as semi-idiot, over whom he has to watch and for whom
he has to provide all through life, but may, whatever be his
circumstances, place him where his intellect can be cultivated,
and where he can be taught some useful art or trade, and made
capable of taking care of himself and ministering to his own
necessities, because instead of an incumbrance and regret, an
independent worker and a pride.

De l' Epee having devoted himself for twenty-nine years to
his task with a zeal and disinterestedness never supposed in this
or any other field of philanthropy, died on the 2d Dec., 1789,
at the age of sixty-seven years. A few years after the death
of De l' Epee, the Royal Institution of Paris was established,
to the direction of which, Roche Ambrose Sicard, a native of
Toulouse, and a pupil of De l' Epee, was placed. It was the
endeavor of this instructor to carry out and perfect the views
of his master and predecessor. Of Sicard's success we have a
striking example in the case of Laurent Clerc, whose ability to
read and write both French and English with great facility and

correctness, shows to what perfection De l' Eppee and Sicard had reduced the science of deaf mute instruction. From the French school of De l' Eppee and Sicard, deaf mute instruction as practiced in America, has its origin.

A little deaf mute girl, the daughter of Dr. Coggswell, a physician of Hartford, attracted the attention of Thos. H. Gallondet, himself a Frenchman by descent. As De l' Eppee's sympathies were aroused in favor of the twin sisters, so Gallondet's were awakened by the spectacle of a beautiful child cut off from the world by an incurable defect. Gallondet's efforts to make her understand words by signs were to some extent successful, and he determined to visit Europe and perfect himself in the methods then in successful operation, and that he might be enabled to relieve the unfortunate in this country. His first application was made to the deaf mute instructors in Great Britain, but the sordid and narrow minded selfishness of the British teachers, compelled him to go to France. The venerable Sicard freely imparted all the information in his power, and gave him all the facilities presented by the Parisian Institution to acquire a perfect acquaintance with the art. It was well he was forced to go to France, as the method of instruction there is much more simple, natural and philosophical than the method invented and practiced by Braidwood and his successors. He was fortunate too, in France, in enjoying the advantage of daily intercourse with Bebian and Clere, the greatest masters of the language of pantomime. Mr. Gallondet had the rare good fortune to secure the services of Laurent Clere as an associate in his contemplated labors in America. Laurent Clere was a deaf mute instructed by Sicard, who attained to great perfection in the sign language and learned to read and write fluently in several languages. He has exercised a very happy influence on the instruction of the deaf and dumb in this country, and it is mainly owing to his and Gallondet's improvements on De l' Eppee's system, that the American schools have attained to greater proficiency than the European institutions.

Bebian, who was then associated with Sicard, and who was himself the most accomplished instructor in Europe, said, "that Clere was then both the most distinguished pupil and the ablest professor of the Parisian Institution—its glory and its support."

There are now in the United States more than twenty insti-

tutions, all of which have sprung from the American institution
for deaf mutes, established at Hartford by the efforts of Gallou-
det and Clerc, in May, 1817.

The earliest intimation we have of an effort in behalf of the
deaf and dumb in Alabama is an act of the General Assembly
at the session of 1851-2, setting apart $5000 to be expended in
instructing the indigent deaf and dumb in the State. This sum
was put under the control of the Governor, subject to many re-
strictions, with no instructions to employ any particular instructor, or to make any definite arrangements providing for the
establishment of a permanent school. In 1852 a school was in
operation in Autauga, which continued only for a short time.
Of the history of its opening, progress and close, we know
nothing. The Legislature of '53-4, '55-6, re-passed the act of
'51-2, but we do not know that any advantage resulted to the
cause therefrom during those years, or that a school was any-
where in the State. At the session of 1857-8, in addition to
the usual appropriation, the Governor and Superintendent of
Public Schools were appointed special Commissioners to select
a location, procure a house, and employ a competent corps of
teachers to instruct deaf mutes in this State. The Commissioners selected Talladega as the location, and rented this building,
erected for and formerly used by the East Ala. Masonic Female
Institute, for the use of the school. They also procured the
services of the present competent and efficient Director, Dr. J.
H. Johnson, who had been engaged for many years in the Georgia Institution.

The Alabama Institution for the Deaf and Dumb, was organized here early in October, 1858. In July, 1859, the visiting
committee at the close of the first year, report that twenty-two
pupils had been in attendance during the first year, and that of
these, fourteen were beneficiaries. They also report very favor-
ably of the good order and the rapid progress of the pupils.
At the last session the General Assembly added $20,000 to the
usual appropriation, to purchase a lot and building and organ-
ize a permanent institution, and also $1000 to fit out a suitable
work shop where the pupils might be taught a trade, thus pre-
paring them to take their positions, after acquiring sufficient
education, to mingle intelligently with the world as independent members of society

Too much praise cannot be awarded the members of the last General Assembly for these wise, liberal and statesmanlike appropriations. What could more worthily engage the consideration and demand the aid of a legislative body convened to advance the best interest of the whole State, than an enlarged and liberal policy of instruction, raising up a class of our fellow citizens sunk in hopeless ignorance, heathenism and helplessness, to the full stature of independent, thinking, active men and women and pouring into their souls the light of hope and happiness, giving them a knowledge of the truths of christianity and of the glorious plan of redemption.

The Commissioners, under the requirements of the act above alluded to, purchased this building where the school was already in operation, and the fourteen acre lot upon which it is located. The selection is in every respect a judicious one; this building is spacious and well arranged and adapted for the use to which it will in future be devoted; the situation is healthy and commanding pleasing and diversified scenery.

I cannot close this brief and imperfect history of deaf mute instruction just inaugurated in Alabama, without a passing tribute to the warm and unflagging interest which Gov. Moore, our excellent Chief Magistrate, has from the first manifested in this enterprise. He has been persistent and untiring in his efforts to establish it on a firm and successful basis, and it is owing greatly to his fostering care that so much has been, in a short time, prosperously accomplished. The mutes in Alabama will gratefully remember all he has done for them.

The philanthropist and the christian may equally rejoice and equally applaud this enterprise; the one, that the unfortunate is elevated in the scale of social and intellectual being and a thousand new sources of happiness opened up to him, and the other, that to these earthly blessings are added, a knowledge of the Bible and its blessed teachings, and the ability to fit himself for a higher and holier existence.

It is true we cannot give to the deaf mute the capacity to find delight in music; to listen to the thrilling tones of the orator, or the kindly words of friendship, or "love's low, soft accents murmured in the ear;" but we can ameliorate his unfortunate condition until half its bitterness is forgotten.

There are in the United States alone, more than 12,000 deaf

4

mutes. If we could congregate them all in one silent band, it would give some conception of the extent and importance of this work. Imagine an assembly greater in numbers than the population of Selma and Talladega combined, sunk in utter ignorance of such things as all household words, acknowledging no God, no law, no kindred, no responsibility, and we can form some estimate of the extent and importance of the field of labor of the deaf-mute instructors.

It is a work too that should come home to every heart and house in the land. Deafness is not hereditary; it is a misfortune that may fall on some member of every family. A chance blow may deprive a child of hearing; a typhus, brain or scarlet fever may fasten on its delicate organism and close the ear forever. What mother is there, who may be called upon to press her stricken offspring to her heart, vainly striving to call back this departed sense, forever gone; who will not fervently invoke God's blessing on this enterprise.

We all may have a direct, individual, selfish interest in furthering this good work. And as brothers by a common humanity, to whom nothing can be foreign or indifferent, we should give the warmest wishes of our hearts, and the earnest assistance of our minds and hands to urge on this undertaking, worthy to inspire the noblest intellects; glorious enough to excite the emulation of angels.

TERMS OF ADMISSION.

Persons, able to educate their children, are required to pay or secure to the Board of Trustees, the sum of one hundred and forty dollars per scholastic year, or at that rate for the time they remain in the Institution.

Children, whose parents are unable to educate them, will be received into the Institution, *free of charge for board and tuition.* An affidavit must be made, by some person cognizant of the fact, as to the inability of the parent to pay.

☞ All pupils will be required to come provided with a suitable supply of clothing, or to deposit with the Principal the sum of thirty dollars to supply clothing.

For further information, address "Dr. J. H. JOHNSON, Principal," or "Secretary of the Alabama Institution for Deaf and Dumb," Talladega, Ala.

☞ *Since the foregoing Report was sent to press,* Dr. J. H. JOHNSON *has resigned his position as Captain of the Alabama Rifles, and will resume his position as Principal of the Alabama Institution for the Deaf and Dumb.*

The next Session of the Institution will open on the first Monday in October.

NOTE.—The Secretary's report, as well as the other material of the Catalogue, (exclusive of the reports of the Principal, Steward and Treasurer, and the annual address,) was prepared and arranged, in the absence of Dr. Taylor, Secretary of the Board, by M. H. Cruikshank, Secretary *pro tem.*